DESERT MEDITATIONS

poems by

Barbara Wiedemann

Finishing Line Press
Georgetown, Kentucky

DESERT MEDITATIONS

Copyright © 2018 by Barbara Wiedemann
ISBN 978-1-63534-440-0 First Edition
All rights reserved under International and Pan-American Copyright Conventions. No part of this book may be reproduced in any manner whatsoever without written permission from the publisher, except in the case of brief quotations embodied in critical articles and reviews.

ACKNOWLEDGMENTS

I am grateful to the American Academy in Rome for time and space allowing me to revise these poems. Versions of some of the poems in *Desert Meditations* have appeared in the following publications:

"Afternoon Visit to a Small World," "Homage to Beauty" in *John Clare Society Newsletter*
"Contemplating Time" in *Red Owl*
"Desert Meditation," "Trail to Heart Lake," "A Visitor to the Night World," "Where Buffalo Roam" in *Kerf*
"The Fishing Lesson" in *Alembic*
"Fly Fishing" in *Acorn*
"Following the Snow Leopard," "Magical Realism Comes to the Desert" in *Southern Women's Review*
"Mountains and Pine Forests" in *Lalitamba*
"On Seeing Eternity in the Distance" in *California Quarterly*

Publisher: Leah Maines
Editor: Christen Kincaid
Cover Art: Matthew E. Roberts
Author Photo: Winnie Roberts
Cover Design: Elizabeth Maines McCleavy

Printed in the USA on acid-free paper.
Order online: www.finishinglinepress.com
      also available on amazon.com

Author inquiries and mail orders:
Finishing Line Press
P. O. Box 1626
Georgetown, Kentucky 40324
U. S. A.

Table of Contents

Following the Snow Leopard 1
To Georgia O'Keeffe on Visiting Ghost Ranch 2
Sounds of the Desert near Rio Chama 3
Desert Meditation 4
Magical Realism Comes to the Desert 5
Against Shale Oil Exploration in the Desert 6
Degrees of Purity 7
Homage to Beauty 8
The Dance of the Elk 9
Another Dance 10
Canyon Country 11
Where the Buffalo Roam 12
A Visitor to the Night World 13
Fly Fishing 14
Mountains and Pine Forests 15
The Trail to Heart Lake 16
An Afternoon Visit to a Smaller World 18
The Unschooled Bird Watcher 19
On Seeing Eternity in the Distance 20
Contemplating Time 21
The Rock Garden 22
The Flight of the Brown Pelicans 23
The High Plains of Texas 24
Thresholds 25

For Anita Kemp

Following the Snow Leopard

Living in a small western town
shadowed by a mountain
she's caught up in mundane tasks
grocery shopping, laundry,
social chitchat
but when she lifts her eyes
away from the ordinary
there the mountain
a jagged peak of snow and rock
is still in sunlight
and she knows
that's where she's going,
where she must go.
All she has to do
is follow the trail out of town.

To Georgia O'Keeffe on Visiting Ghost Ranch

I have stood where you have,
seen the same rose and gold colored cliffs,
smelled the sage and juniper,
felt the dry desert air,
and heard the coyotes at dusk.
Now I understand your paintings,
uncluttered and primal,
reduced to the elements.

Sounds of the Desert near Rio Chama

So still the desert is
that you hear
the raven's wings against the air
like a breath exhaling
or maybe like the slow panting of an animal,
a dog perhaps.
So quiet the desert is
that you sometimes hear sounds
like the crackle and pop
of a breakfast cereal
emanate from the juniper and pinyon pines.
You must look closely
to discover the bark-colored locusts
snapping and rubbing
their gossamer wings together.
So still and quiet the desert is
that you find yourself again.

Desert Meditation

Have you ever watched
rain in a desert,
the first drops
before the ground is moist?

The earth releases
a small puff of dust
as each drop
impacts the ground.

Magical Realism Comes to the Desert

With unexpected rain
in southwest Colorado
near the hamlet of Dove
the mundane gives way to the magical
and there it is
a pink horse
glorious in its pinkness,
a horse which might once have been white
before it rolled in the red earth
but only might have been,
one can't ever be sure.

Against Shale Oil Exploration in the Desert

Last year
drought decimated
the cholla and sage and pinyon pines
so this year
shriveled cactus
and dry skeletons of sage
dot the mesa and mountain sides.
Brown needles of pinyons
signal a battle lost,
these hundred year-old pines
defeated by dryness
and opportunistic beetles.

But this year
May thunderstorms
encourage sprouts
from roots of plants
that crumbled to the touch
twelve months ago.
Dwarf evening-primrose
sego lilies and spreading daisies
add color to the high desert.
New shoots of sage
begin at the base of the old
and the few surviving cholla and pinyons
seed the next generations.

Degrees of Purity

Ice crystals sparkle
in the cold early morning air,
Colorado mountain air
that is a degree or two above zero.
Ice crystals so tiny
they float like dust motes
ignoring gravity
shimmering the air.

Homage to Beauty

In the Sangre de Cristo Mountains
at ten thousand feet
there is a small alpine meadow
of only a few acres
with a stream flowing through it
and if you're still
you can hear the water
move over rocks
and if you're really still
you'll see elk at dawn
grazing in the meadow
with its many shades of green
punctuated by patches
of sunny yellow flowers
each with hundreds
of delicate petals.
Botanists call them
by a Latin name—
we call them
dandelions.

The Dance of the Elk

Near Picuris Peak
fifteen miles south of Taos
seven elk graze
on lush May grasses
in the predawn light.
As if by a signal
the elk begin a dance.
One charges
and the confronted
meets the challenge
with a few forward steps,
then pauses and faces away.
Another charges
and the ballet continues
until a circle is formed.
Then as if by another signal
they disappear
into the woods of pine—
all of this before sunrise.

Another Dance

Near Rio Chama are cliffs
of muted golds and reds,
home to ravens,
so black all color is absorbed.
Sometimes two float from a tree
or the sides of the cliffs
flying in unison
gaining altitude
then gliding
and banking into a turn
supported by unseen air currents.
For a brief moment
the ravens face each other
and perhaps touch
initiating a short tumble
and then they repeat the dance.

Must there be a choreographer?

Canyon Country

Silvery lupine
spreading daisy
common paintbrush
in hues from pale orange to red
larkspur
desert phlox
scarlet gilia
blue flax
and others unidentified
color the meadow.
And higher up
still blooming
on this day in early June
are blue irises
and soon will blossom
rock goldenrod.

And to think
I once was content
with the flower shop
on Main Street.

Where the Buffalo Roam

The gentle breathing of buffalo
resembles peaceful snoring
arising out of an echo chamber
or water bubbles being blown in a pitcher.
The soothing low-pitched sound
emanates from the extended family
of massive bulls, cows and their young.
The hum is constant
but there is also the slurping sound
of the light-colored calves
who follow their sucking
by a hard nudge bringing down more milk.
And there are the sounds of the dominant bulls
sniffing possible mates
and intimidating youthful challengers
but not the white birds that alight on their backs.
The Tetons change color as the sun shifts
but the hum is constant,
connecting the herd.

A Visitor to the Night World

At twilight this summer evening
in the sage-dotted high desert
north of Shoshone, Idaho,
two owls hunt
circling gliding
ten feet off the ground,
soundless with their soft feathers,
one diving at a rabbit
but veering off.

As I watch not moving
they fly near,
sometimes directly at me
and I can see into their deep eyes.
I, by being still, honor them
and they, by hunting, honor me.

Fly Fishing

Two entrepreneurs
with colorful plaid shirts
buttoned over their girth—
fly fishermen for the weekend—
stand in a dory,
maneuvered by a hired guide
who wades in the fifty-five degree current.

No graceful arches of line,
but flat slaps against the water,
no gentle landing of the cutthroat trout,
but snapped lines
and tangles in the lodgepole pines
should the guide absentmindedly
in his boredom move too close to the bank.

Do they notice
the emerald green water
of Henry's Fork
as it flows through the canyon
with its walls of volcanic rock?
Do they notice
the bald eagle overhead
also fishing,
or the grey heron
motionless on the bank?

Earlier I had seen another angler
dressed in beige and grey
sitting on a boulder
bent over tying a fly,
back rounded like the river rocks.
Twice I looked before I could see him clearly.

Mountains and Pine Forests

I
In the Idaho mountains near Silver City
exposed rock
resembling the backs of dragons
mark the mountain ridges,
and on the steep slopes
purple stalks of lupine
orange-red Indian paint brush
purple asters
and white and yellow of unknown others
struggle unaware.

Noticing all
but unnoticed
a woman hikes with a dog.

II
The ten thousand foot peaks of the Sisters
are glimpsed through ponderosa pines
with red brown trunks etched with black,
the ground hidden by needles and cones,
their scent released by the sun's warmth.
Manzanita with waxy green leaves
satiny bark the color of cinnamon
other shrubs resembling sage
but not sage
find life below the pines.

Grateful
for the shadows
and the stillness
of the forest,
she does not move.

The Trail to Heart Lake

Even the sixty-three hundred foot
Black Butte is insignificant
with Mt. Shasta to its right.
Snow-covered Mt. Shasta,
its silence only temporary,
deserves the legends
of those who honor it.
Watching or perhaps waiting,
I sit on granite
two hundred million years old,
a magma outcropping,
in an ancient sea bed.
Seven hundred feet below me
is Castle Lake,
left by a receding glacier,
the same that carved
Heart Lake behind me.

Into the lake I step
expecting the cold of melting snow
but its waters are cool silk
against my skin.
My clothes left on a rock await me,
my body soon to be warmed
by the sun and rock
soon to be chilled
by the breezes of the mountains,
the same breezes that blend
the scents of the blossoming shrubs
into one sweetness
on this first of July
but still a spring day on the mountain
where the only sounds are the insects,

the bird's wing against the air,
and the wind moving through
the Western White Pine
and across my ear.

Should I taste the nectar
that attracts the bees
or the snow left in small patches?
Or are four senses pleasured enough?

An Afternoon Visit to a Smaller World

The snake,
eighteen inches
pencil thin
gray and beige stripes,
fits itself
into the slight crevice
of a gray and beige rock,
a foot or so from shore.
There it suns itself
joined by blue-bodied dragonflies.
Slowly the snake
s-curves onto a branch
gently swayed by wind waves.
There it waits and stares
into the region beneath the surface,
so still
flies crawl along its length.
Its orange tongue
tastes the water
and by tasting it
senses prey,
or so it seems.
A golden shiner,
just a minnow really,
ventures near,
a sudden lunge
a miss
and the snake
resumes its wait.
Finally
unnourished
it curls back on itself
to regain its island rock.

I continue my walk along Castle Lake
and when I return the snake is gone—
at least to me.

The Unschooled Bird Watcher

There it is again
a reddish brown hummingbird
the whir of its wings announces it.
My personal tick list would be high
I've traveled the world,
been to beaches and grasslands,
mountain tops and canyons,
deserts and rain forests
and quietly sat
absorbed by the surroundings
but all I can say is,
it's a blue and grey bird
or it makes a clicking noise
or there are two brown cranes
in a meadow near Mt. Lassen.
Still they bring me pleasure
but I would see more if I knew more.
And now in the mountains near the Rogue River
is another bird singing to me
a common looking brown bird
but an uncommonly beautiful song.

On Seeing Eternity in the Distance

The snowy slopes of Mt. Hood rise above the horizon
seemingly floating above the mountain's dark base
that blue-grey tree-covered part
that fades into the hazy backdrop of the sky.
The clouds touch the snow-capped peak
claiming it for the heavens
releasing it from gravity.

Contemplating Time

The moon in its last quarter
is visible directly above the summit of Mt. Hood
on this morning of the twenty-ninth day of July.

On the north slope
the snow compacted
shimmers blue
in the crevasses.
I wonder,
am I witnessing
the birth of a new glacier
or the death of an old?

The moon has moved off center
but the mountain remains
unchanged to my eye.

The Rock Garden

Purple pin cushion,
baby's breath, yellow asters
and pink sweet pea
these are the names that I know
and I bestow them
on these wild flowers
on the Oregon hillside
in the Siskiyou National Forest,
these flowers that emerge
from a jumble of rocks
pushed aside by a bulldozer
during some road construction,
these flowers finding sustenance
and being so beautiful
out of so little.

The Flight of the Brown Pelicans

I went for a walk
on the beach today.
The Pacific waves
were coming in high
breaking once
a few hundred feet out
and then swelling again
to crash on the steeply angled shore.

Brown pelicans,
not the more common white,
flying in a straight line
one behind the other,
approach the smooth face of the wave,
then glide, rising as it crests,
then over to the next one,
soaring the waves
as hawks do mountains.

I would join them
if I could.

The High Plains of Texas

About as far west as you can go
in the Texas Panhandle
are towns with names like
Muleshoe, Circle Back, and Needmore,
names that tell a history.
Needmore I drive through—
a few houses, no stores or a gas station
an abandoned co-op gin—
Needmore perhaps needs more.
But on the other hand
you would have your family, a few friends,
a livelihood from the fields of the high plains
and just south of town
one hundred thousand sand hill cranes
winter every year.
So, does anyone need more?

Thresholds

The door is always there
multiple doors really
opening in all directions.
But most keep them closed
often even locked
afraid to venture out
to move beyond the ordinary
into the unknown
but the possibility is always there.
And once on the other side
you wonder what took so long
why you hesitated
and the next time
it is easier.

Barbara Wiedemann, professor emerita at Auburn University at Montgomery, taught American literature and creative writing. Since her retirement, she has done more of what she has always loved, namely writing and traveling, the traveling often being an inspiration for her writing. So her first chapbook, *Half-Life of Love*, arose out of her time spent in the West where she goes to escape the hot and humid summers of her hometown, Montgomery, Alabama. Her third chapbook, *Death of a Pope and Other Poems*, found its catalyst in the time she has spent in Rome, spread over the past twenty years as a Visiting Artist at the American Academy in Rome.

Her second chapbook, *Sometime in October*, was in a sense also based on travel, but for this she went back in time to the stories of her family. Wiedemann grew up in the rural areas of New York State, in the Finger Lakes region, where she and her sisters spent days climbing trees, digging in the muddy bank of a pond, roaming the hills then often calling from a neighboring town for their mother to pick them up, and in the winter sledding, ice skating, and building snow caves—a lot of unstructured time spent outdoors but it perhaps formed who Wiedemann would later become. After high school in Horseheads, she went to college at SUNY Buffalo where she majored in English focusing on British literature because she liked to read. After a few peripatetic years she completed her education at University of South Florida where she received her Masters and Ph.D., focusing on modern and contemporary American literature, because she still liked to read. Then she spent over twenty-five years at Auburn University at Montgomery where she tried to instill in her students a love of reading.

Since her retirement in 2015, she has hiked the Pacific Crest Trail, spending five months backpacking, starting in Campo at the border of Mexico and except for a few skipped sections, reaching within two hundred miles of the Canadian border where she was stopped by fire closures. Her dog Angel, an energetic mix of blue heeler and catahoula, was her companion, keeping her from being lonely during those days when she didn't see anyone and warning her when there was a rattlesnake on the trail or a bear in the woods. Then there was some time spent in Rome where she ran her first (and only) marathon and incidentally where she revised the poems in the chapbook, *Desert Meditations*. And because she loves to travel, there have been recent trips to Bulgaria and Nepal and a planned-for trip to Greece.

www.ingramcontent.com/pod-product-compliance
Lightning Source LLC
LaVergne TN
LVHW041515070426
835507LV00012B/1594